Coffee represents 75% of all the caffeine consumed in the United States.

Cinnamon-Mocha Chip Cookies

1 cup butter or margarine, softened
1 cup packed light brown sugar
1 T instant expresso coffee powder
1 T boiling water
1 t vanilla
1 egg
2 cups all-purpose flour
1 t baking soda
1 t ground cinnamon
¼ t salt
1 package (12 oz.) milk chocolate chips
1½ cups coarsely chopped walnuts

Preheat oven to 375°. Line cookie sheets with parchment paper or leave ungreased. Cream butter and sugar in large bowl until smooth. Dissolve coffee powder in water. Add to creamed mixture with vanilla and egg; beat until light. Combine flour, baking soda, cinnamon and salt in small bowl. Blend into creamed mixture until smooth. Stir in chocolate chips and walnuts. Drop by rounded tablespoonfuls 3″ apart onto cookie sheets. Bake 7 to 9 minutes or until just firm in center. Cool 3 minutes on cookie sheet, then remove to wire racks to cool completely. Makes 3 dozen.

Finished Size 65½″ x 85½″ 165 blocks 5″ x 5″

Blocks on pages 22 and 23, photo on page 9.

Fabric (based on 42″ width)

Assorted colorful scraps for stars, square-in-a-square centers, nine-patch squares	3 yds.
Blue/green plaid for square-in-a-square, nine-patch rectangles	2¼ yds.
Assorted golds for square-in-a-square	1½ yds.
Border 1 - red	⅝ yd.
Border 2 - assorted scraps	¾ yd.
Border 3 - blue/green plaid	¾ yd.
Backing (horizontal seams)	4¼ yds.
Binding - red	⅝ yd.

Template or Rotary Cutting

This quilt can be entirely template cut or rotary cut, or a combination of the two. Remember to add ¼″ seam allowances if making templates for machine piecing (see page 2).

Piece/Template	Color/Fabric	Quantity	Rotary Cut Size
NINE-PATCH BLOCKS (make 83)			
#1	scraps	1079	1½″ x 1½″
#2	blue/green	332	1½″ x 3½″
SQUARE-IN-A-SQUARE BLOCKS (make 74)			
#3	scraps	74	3″ x 3″
#4	blue/green	148*	2⅝″ x 2⅝″*
#5	golds	148*	3⅜″ x 3⅜″*
VARIABLE STAR BLOCKS (make 8)			
#3	scraps	8	3″ x 3″
#4	scraps	16*	2⅝″ x 2⅝″*
#6	scraps	32*	2⅛″ x 2⅛″*
#7	scraps	32	1¾″ x 1¾″
Border 1	red	7	2½″ x 42″
Border 2	scraps	280	1½″ x 1½″
Border 3	blue/green	8	2½″ x 42″
Binding	red	8	2½″ x 42″

*Note: These pieces are squares that will be cut in half to make triangles in double the quantity listed.

Directions

1. Rotary cut or template cut the pieces listed in the chart above.
2. Piece blocks as illustrated.
3. Following quilt layout diagram, arrange blocks into fifteen rows of eleven each. Stitch blocks into rows and then stitch rows together. Press well.
4. Piece Border 1 strips end to end. Measure and cut correct lengths for sides. Stitch to quilt. Repeat for top and bottom.
5. Piece Border 2 squares into two strips of 79 squares each. Piece these strips to sides.
6. Piece Border 2 squares into two strips of 61 squares each. Piece these strips to top and bottom.
7. Piece Border 3 strips end to end. Measure, cut, and stitch as in Step 4.
8. Layer with backing and batting. Quilt as desired. Bind.

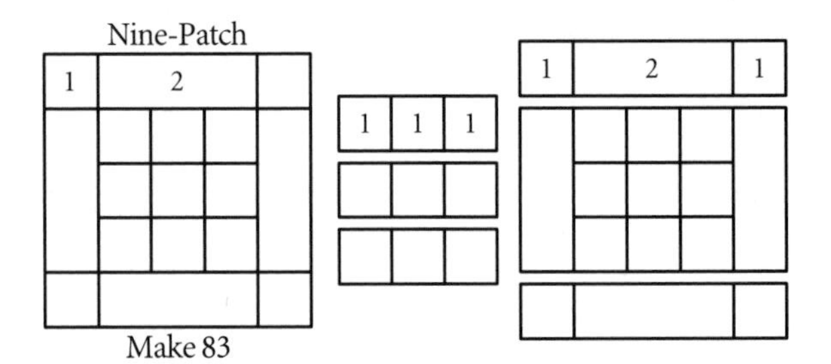

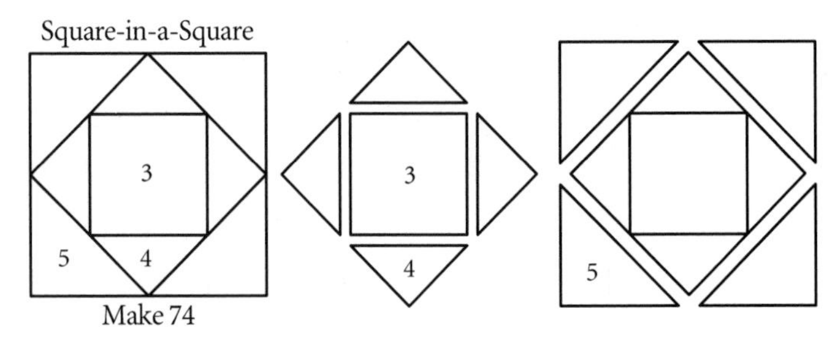

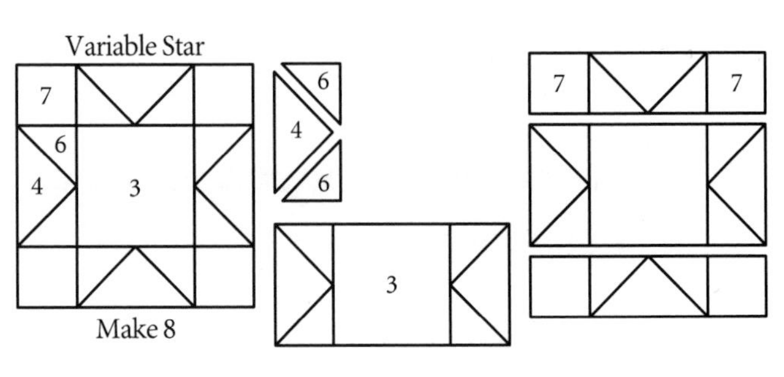

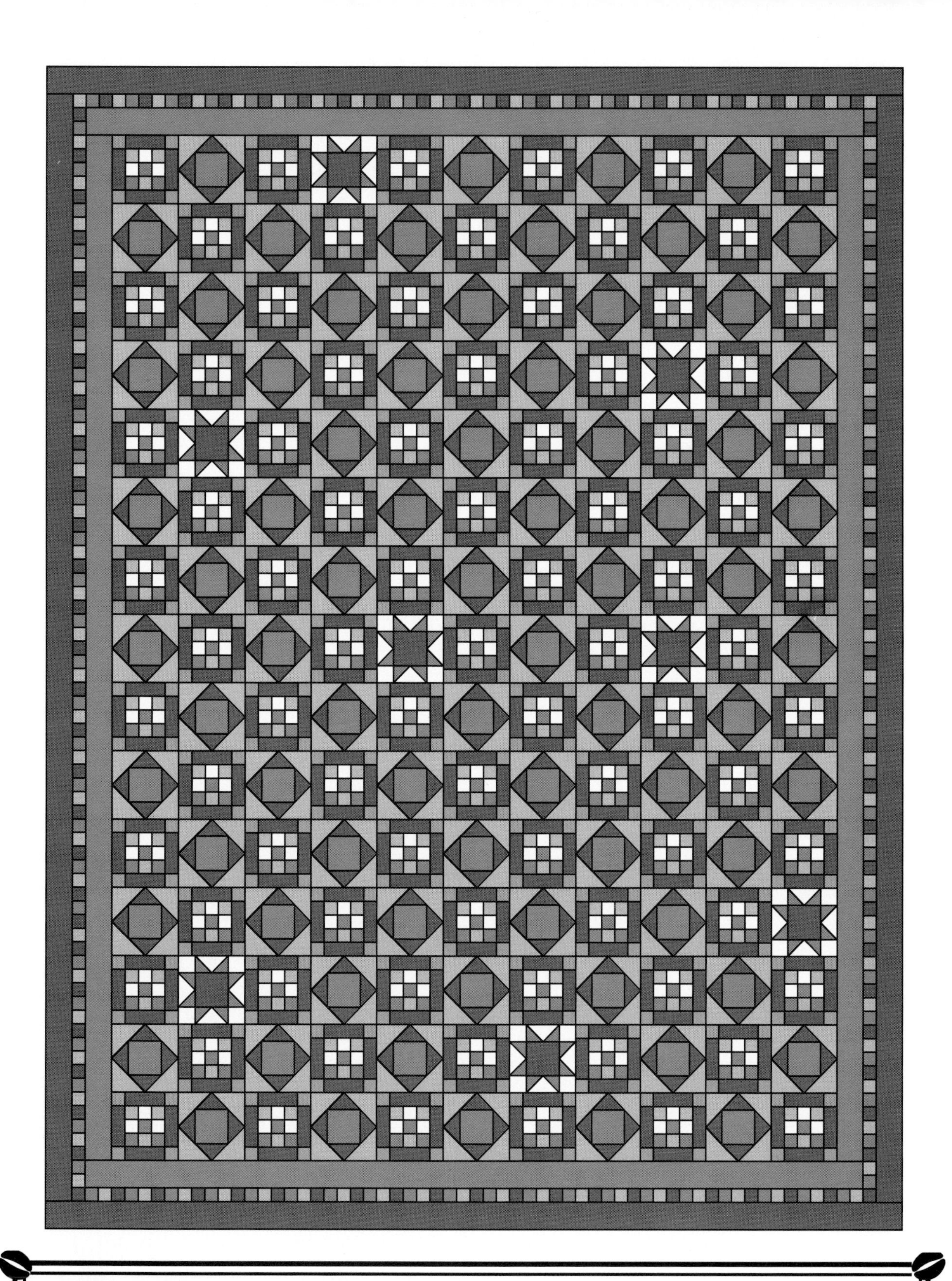

Coffee Sauce

1 cup granulated sugar
1⅔ cups extra-strength coffee, warm
2 T cornstarch, 2 T unsalted butter, ⅓ t salt

In a heavy skillet, melt the sugar slowly, stirring often, until the sugar is a light amber color, about 5 minutes. Slowly add 1⅓ cups coffee, sitrring constantly. Be prepared for a lot of steam!

In a small bowl, blend the cornstarch and the remaining ⅓ cup coffee until smooth. Stir the mixture into the hot coffee/sugar mixture. Continue cooking over low heat and stir until the sauce boils and thickens, about 8 to 10 minutes. Remove from heat and stir in butter and salt until blended. Serve warm over ice cream. To serve chilled, omit the butter. Makes 2 cups.

Finished Size 32½″ x 40½″ 20 blocks 5″ x 5″

Block on page 24, photo on page 14.

Materials (fabrics based on 42″ width)

Suit scraps	1 yd.
Tie or tie-like fabrics	½ yd.
Shirt or shirt-like fabrics	⅝ yd.
Backing	1 yd.
Binding	⅜ yd.
Shirt buttons	60

Template & Rotary Cutting

This quilt requires some template cutting. We have provided rotary cutting sizes for pieces not needing templates. Remember to add ¼″ seam allowances if making templates for machine piecing (see page 2).

Piece/Template	Color/Fabric	Quantity	Rotary Cut Size
#1	tie fabric	40	NA
#2	tie fabric	20	1½″ x 1½″
#2	shirt fabric	20	1½″ x 1½″
#3	shirt fabric	20/20 rev.	NA
#4	shirt fabric	20/20 rev.	NA
#5	shirt fabric	20	1½″ x 3½″
#6	suit fabric	40	2″ x 5½″
#7	suit fabric	40	2″ x 8½″
Binding	suit fabric	4	2½″ x 42″

Directions

1. Template cut and /or rotary cut the pieces listed in the chart above. Note that half of the #3 and #4 pieces need to be cut in reverse. Flip template over to cut the reverse pieces.
2. Piece the 20 blocks as illustrated. Be sure to set iron to an appropriate setting if using fabrics other than 100% cotton.
3. Piece #6 rectangles to sides of blocks and #7 rectangles to tops and bottoms.
4. Following the quilt layout diagram, arrange the blocks into five rows of four blocks each.
5. Stitch blocks into rows and then stitch rows together. Press well.
6. Stitch buttons in position.
7. Layer with backing and batting. Quilt as desired. Bind.

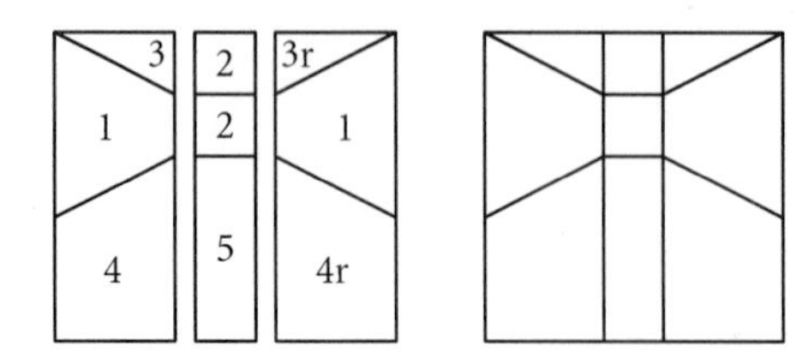

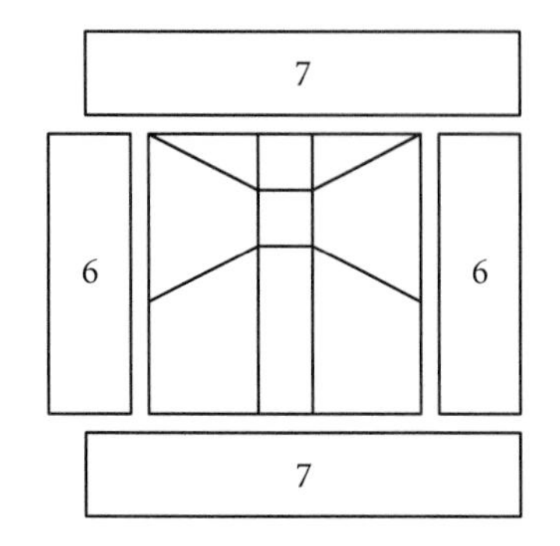

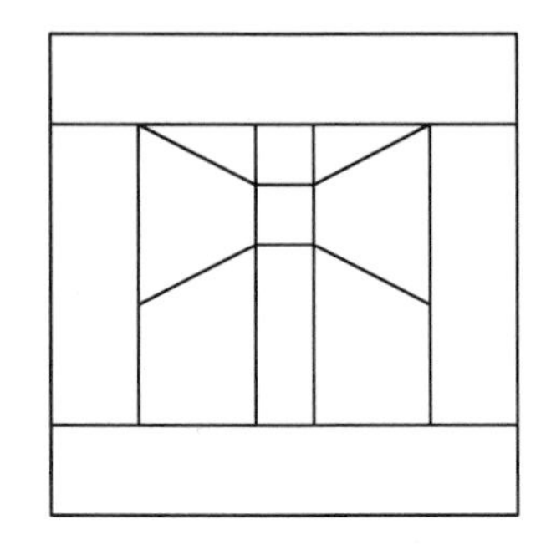

Small Tie Pillow Finished Size 10″ x 10″

Block on page 24, photo on page 14.

You will need:

- one completed Shirt & Tie block (directions on page 6)
- two strips 3″ x 5½″ for side border
- two strips 3″ x 10½″ for top and bottom border
- 10½″ square for backing
- polyester fiberfill

1. Add borders to block as illustrated.
2. Place right side of block down on right side of backing fabric. Stitch around block, leaving a 4″ opening along one side.
3. Turn right side out, stuff firmly, and whipstitch closed.

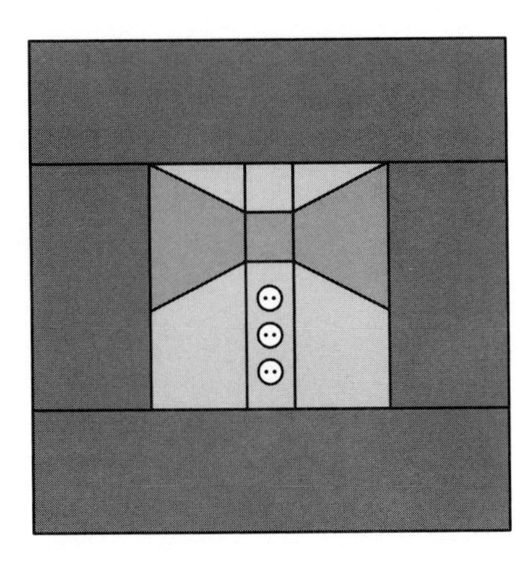

Chewy Coffee Brownies (low fat)

1½ cups firmly packed dark brown sugar
½ cup reduced-calorie stick margarine
2½ T instant coffee granules
1 T vanilla extract
2 egg whites
1 egg
2 cups all-purpose flour
2 t baking powder
⅛ t salt
½ cup semisweet chocolate morsels
vegetable cooking spray

Combine sugar, margarine, and coffee granules in a small saucepan. Place over low heat; cook for 4 minutes or until margarine melts and the mixture is smooth, stirring frequently.

Combine sugar mixture, vanilla, egg whites, and egg; beat at low speed until smooth.

Combine flour, baking powder, and salt; gradually add to creamed mixture, beating well. Stir in chocolate morsels. Spread batter into a 13 x 9-inch baking pan coated with cooking spray. Bake at 350° for 18 minutes; let cool in pan. Makes 2 dozen.

Photo Transfer Pillow Finished Size 16″ x 16″

Blocks on pages 23 and 24, photo on page 14.

You will need:

- one completed Shirt & Tie block (directions on page 6)
- one completed Coffee Time block (directions on page 2)
- one 5½″ x 5½″ photo transfer block of Wall Street Journal
- one 5½″ x 5½″ photo transfer block of comics
- six strips 2½″ x 5½″ for sashing
- three strips 2½″ x 16½″ for sashing
- small scraps of fabric & fusible web for steam
- 16½″ square for backing
- polyester fiberfill

1. Have a section of the Wall Street Journal and a comic strip transferred to fabric. See Photo Transfer Information below.
2. Stitch blocks together and add sashing strips as illustrated.
3. Draw steam on fusible web. Fuse to fabric. Cut out and fuse to pillow as illustrated. Machine applique if desired.
4. Place right side of pillow down on right side of backing fabric. Stitch around block, leaving a 4″ opening along one side.
5. Turn right side out, stuff firmly, and whipstitch closed.

Photo Transfer Information

If you can't find a print shop in your area to make a photo transfer, send us your original/photo and we will reproduce and transfer it to your white fabric ready to be made into a one-of-a-kind pillow. Photos are not ruined by this process. Please send SASE for pricing and information on preparing photos and fabric to Great American Quilt Factory, Inc., Dept. PP-POS 23, 8970 E. Hampden Ave., Denver, CO 80231.

I Like My Coffee Black

Finished Size 14″ x 21″ 6 blocks 7″ x 7″

Cup pattern on page 24, photo on back cover.

Materials

Black felt (72″ wide)	½ yd.
Felt squares in 14 colors: bright red, dark red, wine, plum, light gold, dark gold, medium purple, dark purple, light blue, dark blue, moss green, green, rust, and cream	1 each
Pearl cotton #5 in colors to match felt including black	1 skein each
Freezer paper	½ yd.
Fabric glue	

Directions

1. Cut six 9″ black squares. The extra fabric allows for stretching while doing the blanket stitch.
2. On freezer paper, draw six sets of pieces for cups. Cut pieces apart. Do not cut on lines.
3. Press freezer paper patterns to felt. Cut pieces out and remove freezer paper.
4. Center cups and hearts on 9″ squares. Note that the direction of half of the cups has been reversed so that all handles face toward outer edge.
5. Tack each piece into place with a dab of glue. Keep glue away from edges.
6. Blanket stitch around each piece with a matching color.
7. Trim blocks to 7″ square.
8. Cut 14″ x 21″ rectangle of black felt. Place blocks on felt. Baste in place.
9. Cross stitch the blocks together. Blanket stitch outside edge.

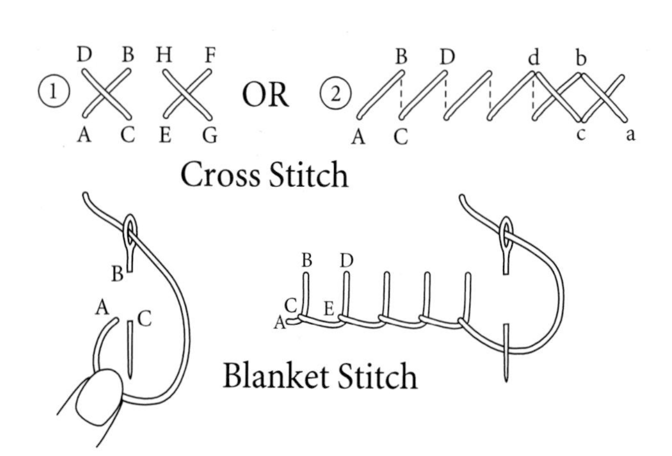

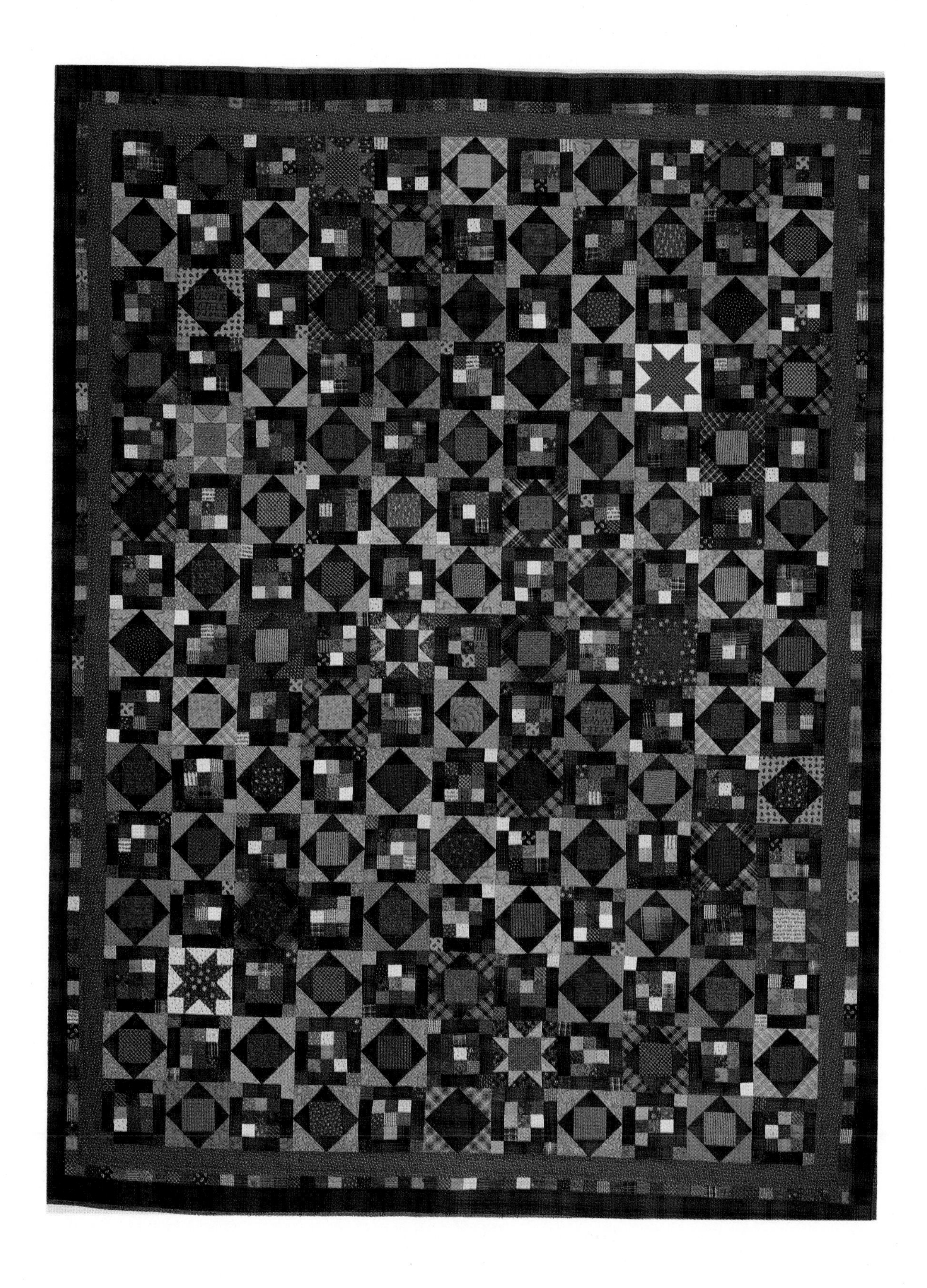

Four-Cup Limit & Sampler Pillow

Quilt Lover's Coffee

The five pieced blocks in this book go together beautifully. We put together this sampler quilt as an added bonus. Gather scraps of blues, browns, and beiges. Make six each of the five 5″ blocks, referring to pages 2-6. Stitch together, referring to photo. Borders are cut 3½″ wide.

Wall Street Journal

ROAST IT!
GRIND IT!
FILTER IT!
BREW IT!
DRINK IT!

Razzmatazz

Accessories

Tea Towels Finished Size 18″ x 25″

Cup pattern on page 24, photo on page 15.

You will need:

- ¾ yd. fabric for 2 towels
- 5″ x 5″ scraps for cups, saucers, hearts, & letters
- Fusible web

1. Cut a rectangle 18½″ x 25½″ for each towel. Narrowly hem all four edges of rectangle.
2. Fold rectangle lengthwise into thirds and press in creases.
3. Draw applique pieces on smooth side of fusible web (to make them like the ones in the photo, reverse handles). Cut pieces apart (do not cut on lines).
4. Fuse pieces to fabrics, following manufacturer's directions. Cut out pieces on lines; peel off paper backing.
5. Using creased lines for a guide, arrange pieces and fuse into place. Place cups approximately 2½-3″ from bottom.
6. Blanket stitch around each piece by hand or machine.

Potholders Finished Size 7½″ x 7½″

Blocks on pages 22-24, photo on page 15.

You will need:

- One completed 5½″ Coffee Time or Variable Star block
- Two strips 1½″ x 5½″ for border
- Two strips 1½″ x 7½″ for border
- One strip 1½″ x 4″for loop (optional)
- One 7½″ square for backing
- Three 7½″ squares of cotton batting

1. Stitch border strips to 5½″ block.
2. Press loop strip in half lengthwise. Press raw edges toward center. Stitch.
3. Layer batting squares, background square right side up and pieced block right side down. Insert loop in one corner between fabric layers.
4. Stitch around potholder, leaving a 3″ opening for turning.
5. Trim corners. Turn right side out and whipstitch closed.
6. Quilt ⅜″ from outside edge to keep pieces from shifting. Quilt remainder of block as desired.

Gift Jars

Cup pattern on page 23, photo on page 15.

You will need:

- Scraps for lid and tag
- Fusible web

1. Cut a circle of heavy paper the same size as the inner metal lid. Fuse fabric to the paper. Lay it on top of the metal lid and screw the band on as usual.
2. Gift tag: Bond fabric cup to heavy paper and trim to cup edges. Tie a string through handle.

Nine-Patch Template

Basket Liner Finished Size 23½″ x 23½″

Alphabet on page 24, photo on front cover.

You will need:

- ¾ yd. each of two fabrics
- ⅛ yd. for letters
- Scraps of red and yellow for hearts and stars
- Fusible web

1. Cut fabric into two 24″ squares. Place right sides together.
2. Stitch around squares, leaving a 4″ opening. Turn right side out and press well.
3. Trace letters, hearts and stars on smooth side of fusible web. Cut pieces apart (do not cut on lines). We used the words Cafe au Lait, Cafe Latte, Irish Coffee, and Cafe Royale.
4. Fuse to desired fabrics. Cut pieces out on lines. Peel off paper backing.
5. Place words around the corners with a star separating the words. Between the words on the four sides, we placed five red hearts and one yellow heart.

Sampler Pillow Finished Size 15″ x 15″

Blocks on pages 23 and 24, photo on page 10.

You will need:

- One completed Coffee Time block, one completed Shirt & Tie block, one nine-patch block using template below, and one 5½″ plain block
- Two strips 3″ x 10½″ for top & bottom borders
- Two strips 3″ x 15½″ for side borders
- Scrap of red fabric for hearts
- 15½″ square for backing
- Scrap of fusible web, polyester fiberfill

1. Stitch blocks together and add borders as illustrated.
2. Draw hearts on fusible web. Fuse to red fabric. Cut out and fuse to pillow as illustrated. Machine applique if desired.
3. Place right side of pillow down on right side of backing fabric. Stitch around block, leaving a 4″ opening along one side.
4. Turn right side out, stuff firmly, and whipstitch closed.

Finished Size 18¼″ x 30¼″ 6 blocks 7″ x 7″

Cup pattern on page 24, photo on page 11.

Materials (fabrics based on 42″ width)

Cups, saucers, hearts - assorted prints	scraps 5″ x 5″
Block backgrounds - 6 different creams	scraps 8″ x 8″
Letters	⅛ yd.
Background for letters	⅛ yd.
Sashing strips	½ yd.
Backing	⅝ yd.
Binding	¼ yd.
Fusible web	¼ yd.

Template & Rotary Cutting

This quilt requires applique templates. Rotary cutting sizes are given for background, sashing, and binding.

Piece/Template	Color/Fabric	Quantity	Rotary Cut Size
#1, 2, 3, 4, 5, 6	assorted prints	6 each	
Background	creams	6	7½″ x 7½″
Letters backgr.	cream	1	3″ x 15¾″
Sashing strips		8	1¾″ x 7½″
Sashing strips		1	1¾″ x 15¾″
Sashing strips		1	1¾″ x 26½″
Sashing strips		2	1¾″ x 30¼″
Binding		3	2½″ x 42″

Directions

1. Rotary cut the pieces listed in the chart above.
2. Trace the cups, saucers, hearts, and letters onto the smooth side of the fusible web. Cut pieces apart (do not cut on lines). Follow fusible web directions for iron settings and bond the web to the desired prints with the rough side of the web against the wrong side of the fabric. Cut the pieces out on the lines and peel off the paper. Refer to layout diagram and photo for positioning the applique pieces on the blocks. Press and bond into place. Machine applique letters , hearts, and cups, if desired.
3. Following the quilt layout diagram, arrange the blocks and strips and piece together as illustrated.
4. Layer with backing and batting. Quilt as desired. Bind.

The average annual coffee consumption of the American adult is 26.7 gallons, or over 400 cups.

Four Cup Limit

Finished Size 18¼″ x 18¼″ 4 blocks 7″ x 7″

Cup pattern on page 24, photo on page 10.

Materials (fabrics based on 42″ width)

Cups, saucers, hearts - assorted prints	scraps 5″ x 5″
Block background	¼ yd.
Sashing strips	¼ yd.
Backing	⅝ yd.
Binding	¼ yd.
Fusible web	⅙ yd.

Template & Rotary Cutting

This quilt requires applique templates. Rotary cutting sizes are given for background, sashing, and binding.

Piece/Template	Color/Fabric	Quantity	Rotary Cut Size
#1, 2, 3, 4, 5, 6	assorted prints	4 each	
Background	creams	4	7½″ x 7½″
Sashing strips		6	1¾″ x 7½″
Sashing strips		3	1¾″ x 18¼″
Binding		2	2½″ x 42″

Directions

See Quilt Lover's Coffee.

Gateau with Coffee Sauce

CAKE
2 eggs
¼ t salt
1 cup sugar
1 t rum extract
½ cup milk
1 T butter
1 cup flour
1 t baking powder
½ cup drained apricot preserves
½ cup light frozen whipped topping, thawed
Coffee Syrup (recipe follows)
Cream Filling (recipe follows)

Beat eggs until thick and light. Beat in salt and extract. Heat milk and butter to boiling point and beat into eggs. Mix and sift flour and baking powder; beat in. Turn into well greased and floured 9″ cake pan 1½″ deep. Bake at 350° for 35-40 minutes. Remove from pan. Spoon coffee syrup slowly and evenly over surface of warm cake until all is absorbed. Let stand until cool. Split crosswise, carefully, to make two layers. Fill with cream filling. Spread top with preserves, then whipped topping.

COFFEE SYRUP

Combine ½ cup strong coffee and ½ cup sugar. Stir over low heat until sugar dissolves. Boil 3 minutes. Add 1 tsp. rum extract or more to taste.

CREAM FILLING
⅓ cup sugar
¼ cup flour
⅛ t salt
1 cup milk
2 egg yolks, slightly beaten
1 t rum extract

Combine sugar, flour, and salt in top of double boiler. Add milk. Cook and stir over low heat until thickened. Cover and cook ten minutes longer. Add a little hot mixture to egg yolks. Combine with remaining hot mixture and cook 2 minutes longer, stirring constantly. Add flavoring and chill.

Finished Size 28″ x 33″   20 blocks 5″ x 5″

Blocks on page 23, photo on page 16.

Fabric (based on 42″ width)

Assorted red scraps	1 yd.
Black print	1 yd.
Backing	1 yd.
Binding	¼ yd.

Template or Rotary Cutting

This quilt can be entirely template cut or rotary cut , or a combination of the two. Remember to add ¼″ seam allowances if making templates for machine piecing (see page 2).

Piece/Template	Color/Fabric	Quantity	Rotary Cut Size
COFFEE TIME BLOCK (make 1)			
#1	black print	3	⅞″ x 1½″
#2	red scraps	3	⅝″ x 1½″
#3	red scrap	1	3½″ x 3½″
#4	black print	1	1½″ x 3½″
#5	black print	1	1½″ x 5½″
#5	red scrap	1	1½″ x 5½″
#6	black print	2	1½″ x 1½″
VARIABLE STAR BLOCKS (make 19)			
#3	red scraps	19	3″ x 3″
#4	black print	38*	2⅝″ x 2⅝″*
#6	red scraps	76*	2⅛″ x 2⅛″*
#7	black print	76	1¾″ x 1¾″
Border 1	black print	4	1¾″ x 42″
Border 2	red scraps	42*	2⅛″ x 2⅛″*
	black print	42*	2⅛″ x 2⅛″*
Border 3	black print	4	1¾″ x 42″
Binding	black print	4	2½″ x 42″

*Note: These pieces are squares that will be cut in half to make triangles in double the quantity listed.

Directions

1. Rotary cut or template cut the pieces listed in the chart above.
2. Piece the Coffee Time block as illustrated. To make the saucer, stitch the #6 squares onto one #5 rectangle as illustrated. Trim seam allowances and press.
3. Piece 19 Variable Star blocks as illustrated.
4. Following the quilt layout diagram, arrange the blocks into five rows of four blocks each. Stitch blocks into rows, then stitch rows together.
5. Measure and cut Border 1 strips to correct lengths for sides. Stitch to quilt. Repeat for top and bottom.
6. Piece Border 2 triangles into squares and then into two side strips of 22 triangle sets each and two top/bottom strips of 20 triangle sets each. *Be sure to change the direction of the triangles at the midpoint of each border strip.* Piece these strips to sides and top and bottom.
7. Measure, cut, and stitch Border 3 as in Step 5.
8. Layer with backing and batting. Quilt as desired. Bind.

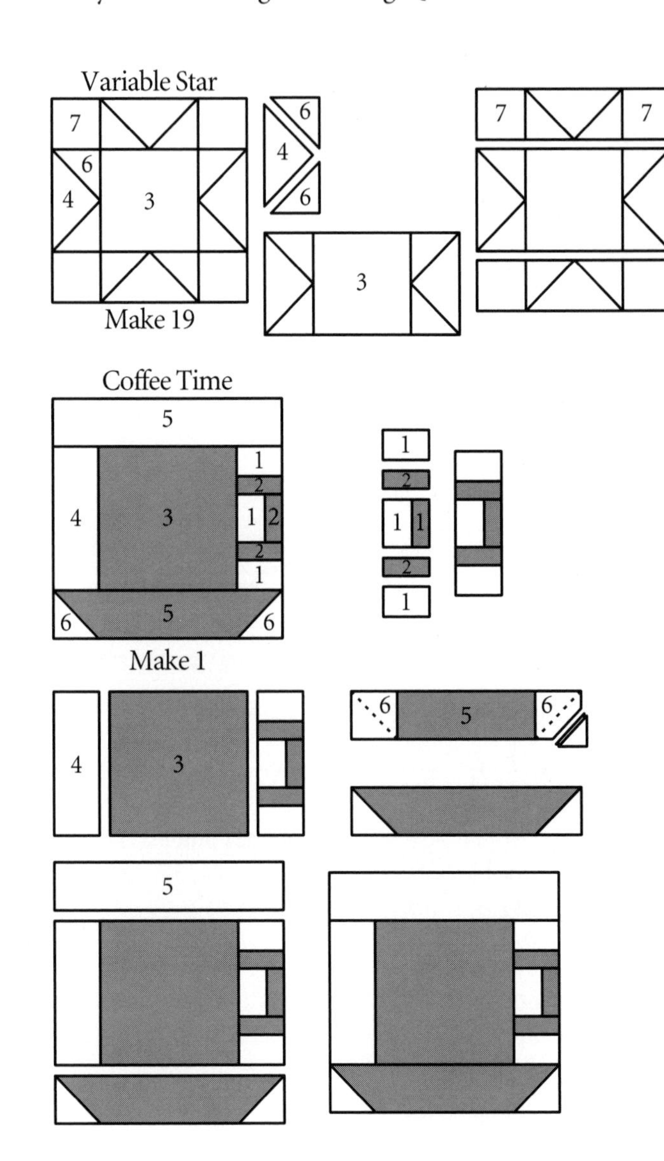

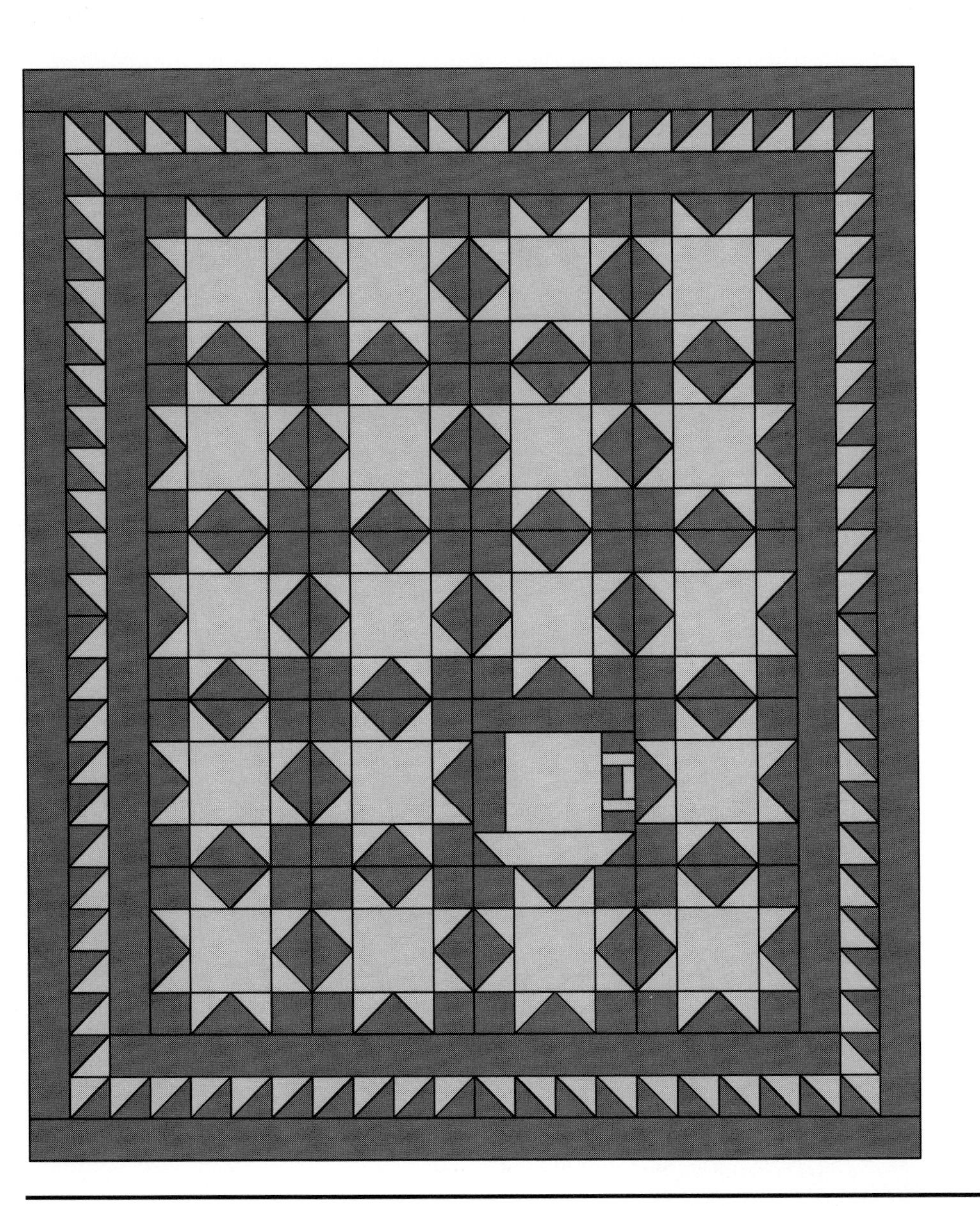

Razzmatazz Latté

Pour ½ oz. each of chocolate and raspberry syrups into a cup. Add expresso. Fill with foamed/steamed milk.

Acidity is the sharp, snappy taste that wakes up your coffee.

Coffee Aroma

Finished Size 23½″ x 9½″

Blocks on page 23, photo on front cover.

You will need:

- Two completed Variable Star blocks, one completed Coffee Time block
- Four strips 2½″ x 5½″ for sashing
- Two strips 2½″ x 23½″ for sashing
- Two strips 2½″ x 42″ for binding
- One rectangle 10″ x 24″ for backing
- ⅛ yd. fabric for letters
- Scrap of red fabric for hearts
- ⅛ yd. fusible web

1. Stitch blocks together and add sashing strips as illustrated.
2. Draw hearts on smooth side of fusible web. Cut pieces apart (do not cut on lines). Fuse to red fabric. Cut out pieces on lines, remove paper, and fuse to block. Machine applique if desired.
3. Layer with backing and batting. Quilt as desired. Bind.

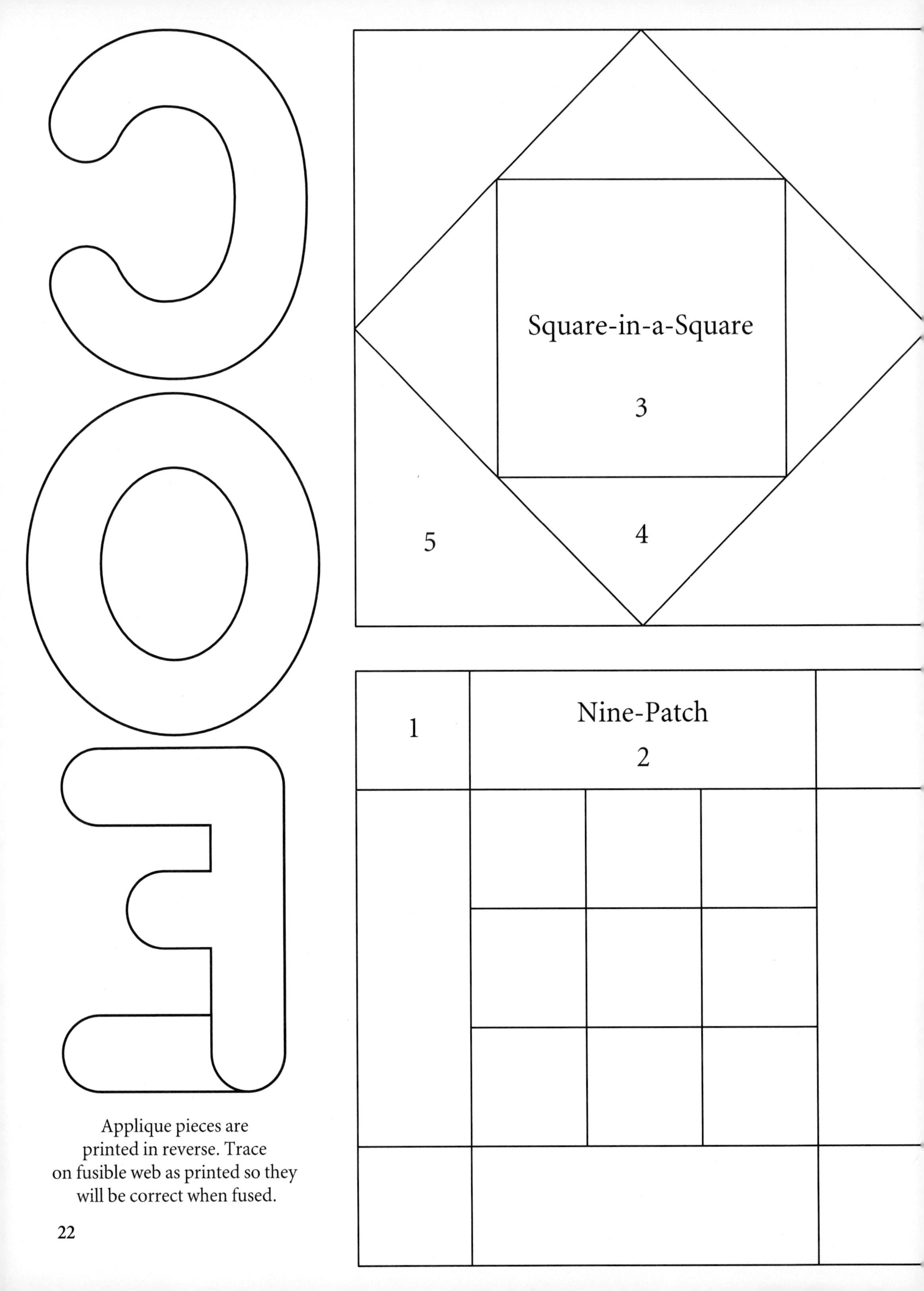

Applique pieces are printed in reverse. Trace on fusible web as printed so they will be correct when fused.

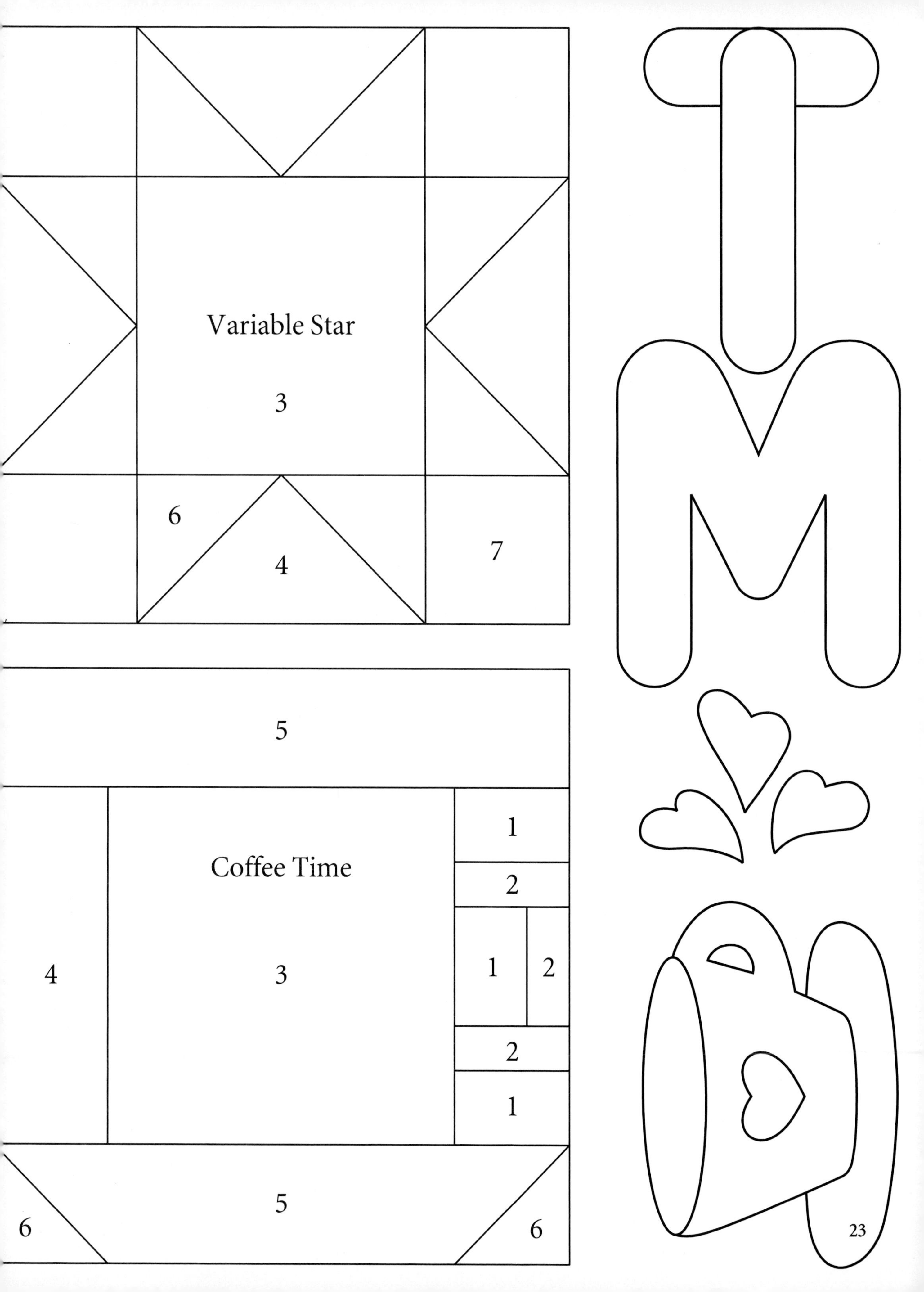
Variable Star
3
6
4
7
5
1
Coffee Time
2
4
3
1
2
2
1
5
6
6

Applique pieces are printed in reverse. Trace on fusible web as printed so they will be correct when fused.